Love

THE SCHOOL OF LIFE
Essential Ideas

Love

Published in 2024 by The School of Life
First published in the USA in 2024
930 High Road, London, N12 9RT

Copyright © The School of Life 2024

Designed and typeset by Myfanwy Vernon-Hunt
Printed in China by Leo Paper Group

A proportion of this book has appeared online at
www.theschooloflife.com/articles

Every effort has been made to contact the copyright holders
of the material reproduced in this book. If any have been
inadvertently overlooked, the publisher will be pleased to
make restitution at the earliest opportunity.

The School of Life publishes a range of books on essential topics
in psychological and emotional life, including relationships,
parenting, friendship, careers and fulfilment. The aim is always
to help us to understand ourselves better – and thereby to
grow calmer, less confused and more purposeful. Discover
our full range of titles, including books for children, here:
www.theschooloflife.com/books

The School of Life also offers a comprehensive therapy service,
which complements, and draws upon, our published works:
www.theschooloflife.com/therapy

www.theschooloflife.com

ISBN 978-1-916753-03-7

10 9 8 7 6 5 4 3 2 1

MIX
Paper | Supporting
responsible forestry
FSC® C020056

Contents

6   Introduction

9   Arguments

13   Attachment Theory

17   Closeness

20   Crushes

23   Dating Apps

27   Emotional Translation

30   Heartbreak

35   Infidelity

39   Kissing

42   Long-Distance Love

45   Long-Term Love

48   Love as Education

51   Love as Generosity

53   Love Me as I Am

56   Loving and Being Loved

59   Monogamy

62   Romantic Disappointment

65   Romantic Instinct

68   Secrets

72   Self-Love

76   Sex

80   Splitting and Integration

83   Sulking

86   The Happy Single

89   Unrequited Love

Introduction

Relationships are perhaps our single greatest source of both happiness and suffering. Unlike people in previous ages, we don't merely seek a partner we can tolerate; we seek someone we can love, usually over many decades, at an intense pitch of desire, commitment and interest. We dream of someone who will understand us, with whom we can share our longings and our secrets, and with whom we can properly be ourselves.

Then the horror begins. We need to understand why. Some of it is because our childhoods leave us with a legacy of trouble relating to others. We have difficulties trusting or being close, achieving the right distance or staying resilient. We cannot comfortably express what we feel and are prone to 'transfer' a lot of emotions from the past on to present-day scenarios where they don't quite belong.

We need to chart our own psyches and offer maps of our madness to partners early on, before we have had the chance to hurt them too much with our behaviour.

Our current relationship difficulties stem in part from a cultural source that we call 'Romanticism'. In the background, we operate with a deeply problematic Romantic picture of what good relationships should be like: we dream of profound intimacy, satisfying sex, an absence of secrets and only a modicum of conflict. This faith in love is touching, but it carries with it a tragic flaw: our expectations turn out to be the enemies of workable mature relationships.

At The School of Life, we are drawn to what we call a Classical approach to love. The Classical view is in certain ways cautious. Classical people pay special attention to what can go wrong around others. Before condemning a relationship, they consider the standard of partners across society and may interpret a current arrangement as bearable, under the circumstances. This view of people is fundamentally, but usefully, dark. Ultimately, everyone is deeply troubled and hard to live with. The only people we can think of as normal are those we don't know very well.

Here are 25 ideas on love that will help us to understand the complexities of relationships and navigate some of the difficulties we will inevitably face in love.

Arguments

There are couples that seem never to argue. Their relationships are marked by enormous outward politeness; they say thank you a lot; they make each other cups of tea; they can look rather horrified when there's a mention of a squabble in someone else's life. It's understandable if they're privately a little pleased with themselves.

But surface harmony isn't, in reality, any reliable sign of health in love because it's impossible to try to merge two lives without regularly encountering deep sources of incompatibility. A lack of arguments is more likely to be a sign that we have given up caring than a superhuman achievement of maturity.

The goal isn't, therefore, to do away with arguments – but to find our way towards their more fruitful variety. We need to learn to argue well, rather than not argue at all.

What then are some of the ideas that might help us have better arguments?

– The single greatest idea that can help us to argue more constructively is to remind ourselves publicly that we are – both of us – by nature deeply imperfect and at points quite plainly mad.

– People concede points not when they're aggressively told they're wrong, but when they feel loved. It is indispensable to preface every criticism with an assurance of our ongoing love.

– People change very slowly, and seldom when they are harassed into doing so. We must strive not to be desperate for change.

– We shouldn't aggravate our frustration by a sense that we have been uniquely cursed in ending up in this relationship. The specifics of why we're in an irritating dispute may be local, but that we are in one is a universal destiny.

– Our partner is only ever frightened, worried and not thinking straight – rather than bad.

– Choose the moment.

– Don't let the relationship die from misplaced 'politeness' or embarrassment. Dare to name the problem, however shocking it sounds.

– It doesn't matter if we're right.

The capacity to be horrible to a partner is a strange – though genuine – feature of love. A relationship has to include the madder, more unreasonable parts of our nature; if we are only ever polite, it's because we have not been made to feel safe. A row may have to be the turbulent passage towards the kind of deeper reconciliation we long for. It can be important to say some wild and hurtful things to halt a drift apart. By foregrounding for a while the most extreme points of conflict, we set up the conditions for reconnecting with larger areas of closeness. We now remember that, despite an evening squabbling like the frightened, foolish, barely semi-rational idiots we are, we love them deeply nevertheless – and will strive with all our will to argue a little more sensibly next time.

Attachment Theory

An unusual realisation that lovers may eventually make is that it is hard to envisage successfully navigating any relationship without some understanding – and mutual discussion of – Attachment Theory.

First developed in England in the 1950s by the psychologists John Bowlby and Mary Ainsworth, the theory proposes that getting close to someone, or – as the technical term has it – 'attached', invariably generates a degree of fear and risk.

Love requires that we surrender our emotional autonomy. A partner may hurt us through indifference or egoism; they may cheat on us; we could grow deeply dependent on them and then be left at a moment of their choosing.

For those among us fortunate enough to have enjoyed consistent and reliable love from our parents in childhood (roughly fifty per cent of the population), the risks of attachment, though always present to some degree, will be manageable. When they experience doubts, securely attached people know how to voice these calmly before they become intolerable. They can bear to ask for reassurance directly. They can lay bare their vulnerability and need without terror of humiliation or mockery.

However, Bowlby and Ainsworth identified two other categories of lovers for whom things will not be so easy –

on account of having endured less reliable and consistent relationships with their early caregivers (and also, as importantly, of never having fully realised this or taken steps to mitigate the after-effects). They proposed that some twenty-five per cent of us are what they termed 'avoidantly attached'; a pattern in which the risks of getting close to someone are inwardly felt to be so great (because they were precisely so in childhood) that a person quickly becomes 'avoidant' – that is, cold, detached and overly independent – in response to challenges. If there is a period of doubt, if it's unclear whether they are still cherished by their partner, an avoidant person will have no inner strength to admit to their fears and then to share their feelings with self-possession. They will simply pull up the drawbridge, claim that they are very busy and announce that they need space. What they absolutely will not do is generously explain that they are feeling abandoned and desperately need a hug. It's a lot easier to go into the next room and watch a long film.

A comparable problem is to be observed in that other problematic category of lover known as the 'anxiously attached' – though here, rather than going cold in response to a perception of emotional threat, a lover will become angry. They will accuse their partner of all manner of flaws, while carefully keeping hidden the one issue they actually have on their minds. They will get accusatory and mean when, in truth, they are sad and scared. They will denigrate their partner rather than touch on the more poignant and horrifying thought: that they love them deeply and are very worried that they are not loved back.

Both anxious and avoidant patterns of behaviour generate predictable storms. Feeling their loved ones going cold or becoming angry, most partners will withdraw in turn – setting off cycles of distress and recrimination.

Fortunately, the dangers associated with avoidant or anxious responses diminish hugely if lovers are able to admit without shame that they are prone to them; if they can explain, perhaps over an early dinner, the temptation to pull off certain antics when they are scared of being abandoned but then don't in fact do so; if they can confess to their fears without getting swept up by the need to act them out.

We don't need our lovers to be sane. We don't need them to be securely attached. What we need, as ever, is an intense mutual commitment to self-awareness, a huge curiosity about our psyches, constant apologies and some reliable maps of human insanity.

Closeness

Even after years with someone, there can be a hurdle of fear about asking for proof that we are wanted – but with a horrible, added complication: we now assume that any such anxiety couldn't possibly exist. This makes it very difficult to recognise our insecure feelings, especially if they have been triggered by a so-called 'small' matter, let alone communicate them to others in ways that would stand a chance of securing us the understanding and sympathy we crave. Rather than requesting reassurance endearingly and laying out our longing with charm, we might instead mask our needs beneath some brusque and hurtful behaviours guaranteed to frustrate our aims. Within established relationships, when the fear of rejection is denied, two major symptoms tend to show up.

Firstly, we may become distant – or 'avoidant'; we disguise our need for our lover.

Secondly, we may become controlling – or 'anxious'; we disguise our vulnerability behind an officious front.

The solution is to normalise a new and more accurate picture of emotional functioning: to make it clear just how healthy and mature it is to be fragile and in repeated need of reassurance, especially around sex. We suffer because adult life posits too robust a picture of how we operate. It tries to teach us to be implausibly independent and invulnerable. It suggests it might not be right to want a partner to show us they still really like us after they have been away for only a few hours, or to want them to reassure us that they haven't gone off us, just on the basis that they didn't pay us much attention at a party and didn't want to leave when we did.

Yet it is precisely this sort of reassurance that we constantly need. We are never through with the requirement for comfort. This isn't a curse limited to the weak and the inadequate. In this area, insecurity is a sign of well-being. It means we haven't allowed ourselves to take other people for granted. It means we remain realistic enough to see that things could genuinely turn out badly and are invested enough to care.

We should create room for regular moments, perhaps as often as every few hours, when we can feel unembarrassed and legitimate about asking for confirmation. 'I really need you; do you still want me?' should be the most normal of enquiries. We should uncouple the admission of need from any associations with the unfortunate and punitively macho term 'neediness'. We must get better at seeing the love and longing that lurk behind some of our and our partner's most frosty, managerial or distant moments.

Crushes

A crush plays out in pure and perfect form the dynamics of the Romantic philosophy of love, with its combustible mixture of limited knowledge, outward obstacles to further discovery, and boundless hope.

When we see someone in the street, on the train or in the library and feel almost at once that they are the answer, we are perhaps not wrong to feel that the stranger has some wonderful qualities, indicated by their eyebrows, quizzical smile or extremely handsome mustard-coloured coat. But our crush ignores a fundamental truth about people that Romanticism blithely ignores: that everyone, even the most apparently accomplished being, is radically imperfect and, were we to spend a long time around them, possibly maddening (even those who have adorable hair or the sweetest way of folding their skirt under them as they sit down on a park bench). We can't yet know what the problems will be, but we can and should be certain that they are there, lurking somewhere behind the facade, waiting for time to unfurl them.

We have to impress this truth upon our Romantic minds – otherwise, in comparison with a crush, every actual relationship we ever have will seem horrendous and doomed. If we truly believe what our imaginations tell us during crushes, we'll have no logical choice other than to break off our partnerships, which are likely to be somewhat disappointing yet deeply real and ultimately 'good enough'.

In order to enjoy a crush, we have to understand that that is what it is. If we think that we are encountering a person who will make us happy, who will be an ideal person to live with and grow old with, we are inadvertently destroying the specific satisfaction that a crush brings. The pleasure depends on our recognising that we are imagining an ideal person, not finding a real one. To crush well is to realise that the lovely person we sketch in our heads is our creation: a creation that says more about us than them. But what it says about us is important. The crush gives us access to our own ideals. We may not really be getting to know another person properly, but we are growing our insight into who we really are.

Dating Apps

For most of human history, relationships were relatively simple for a banal yet immovable reason: it was extremely hard to meet anyone acceptable – and everyone knew it. There were only a few people in the village, travel was expensive and social occasions few and far between.

Our technologists have used their genius to correct these historic obstacles and provide us with unending choice. Meeting someone new is now a constant possibility. But this breakthrough at the level of introduction has obscured an ongoing challenge at the level of ultimate purpose: we may have become easier to meet, but we are not any easier to love.

We remain – each one of us – highly challenging propositions for anyone to take on. All of us are riddled with psychological quirks that serve to render an ongoing relationship extremely problematic: we are impatient, prone to making unjust accusations, rife with self-pity, and unused to expressing our needs in a way that can be understood by others – just to start the list …

That we can meet so many people has beautifully obscured our ugly sides, breeding in us the charming yet misleading idea – which engulfs us any time we hit difficulties – that we are in trouble because we have not until now met 'the right person.' The reason why there is friction and longing has, we tell ourselves, nothing to do with certain stubborn infelicities in our own natures or paradoxes in the human condition as a whole; it is only a matter of needing to hunt further for a more reasonable candidate who will, at last, see things our way.

The promise of choice has drained us of the patience and modesty necessary to grapple with the tensions that are prone to come our way whomever we might be with. We forget that almost everyone is a charming prospect so long as we know nothing about them. Part of what it takes to be ready for love is to imagine the difficulties that we cannot, as yet, know too much about in detail; the bad moods that will lurk behind the energetic smiles, the difficult pasts that lie beneath the lustrous eyes, the tangled psyches that reside beneath a stated love of camping and the outdoors.

Even though there are hundreds of other people we might meet, there are not – in truth – so many people we could really love. Dating apps may have made it infinitely easier to connect but they haven't helped us in any way to be more patient, imaginative, forgiving or empathetic, that is, any more adept at the arts that make any one relationship viable. Most of the issues we experience with a given candidate will therefore show up, in comparable guises, with almost anyone we might stumble upon.

The real work we should be doing isn't – once we have had a reasonable look around – to keep trying to meet new people; it's to get to the root of what makes it hard to live with any one person we could alight upon.

We will be ready for love when we surrender some of our excited sense of possibility and recognise that though we might have many choices, we don't – in reality – have so many options. It may sound dark, but this will, in its own way, be a liberating realisation that can help us redirect our energies away from the exhausting circuit of new encounters towards a search for the kind of mutual emotional maturity on which true love can one day be built.

Emotional
Translation

One of the most deceptive tricks our minds play upon us is to lead us to believe that we know what other people mean just because we can hear their words.

But often what someone is trying to say is very different from what actually comes out of their mouth. We therefore have to undertake a special kind of translation, moving from listening to interpreting.

The need for translation is especially prominent around relationships. Our Romantic culture stresses sincerity and openness, which can make the idea of translation feel like an insult to another person's directness of heart. Yet it may frequently be much kinder and more loving to dig beneath the surface meaning of words in search of a partner's real but more bashful, complex or vulnerable underlying emotional intention.

'I hate you' might not mean this at all; it might be a plea to be noticed and cared for. 'I'm fine' is unlikely to indicate that a person is fine; it is almost always a sign that the prospect of revealing their real complaint and anger has brought on intolerable feelings of weakness and exposure.

In an ideal future, we might wear in our ears little devices of genius that could simultaneously translate people's words into what they actually meant. We would hear (via our discreet, brushed steel appliances) not what they overtly said, but what they were really attempting to communicate.

In the meantime, we must take up the challenge of picking up on hints rather than looking out only for direct statements; we must learn to wisely interpret rather than just listen to one another.

Heartbreak

The intensity and suffering exacted by a heartbreak depends not only on the core fact that we've been left; it also decisively depends on how we've been left. Our hurt can be hugely intensified when we've been left badly – just as it may be rendered a great deal more bearable when we are fortunate enough to have landed on a lover who has learnt the psychologically rich art of mature break-ups.

There are certain things guaranteed to make a break-up worse than it ever needs to be:

Lingering
All decisions around relationships should be taken with the awareness that life is desperately short for both parties.

Collateral accusations
A wise departing lover knows not to accuse the other of more sins than they are guilty of. The wise lover keeps the list of accusations down to the specific problems that necessitated the break-up; they don't use the parting as an occasion to rehearse all that happens to be a bit wrong with us.

Deceptive niceness
The most harmful lovers are those who labour under a misplaced impression that they need to be nice – even

when they are firing us. But there is, in fact, no need for honeyed words; we simply require the basic information and then some privacy to put ourselves back together again. Indeed, ongoing niceness simply confuses us all the more.

Evasiveness
Clumsy lovers are so scared of the news they have to share with us, they cannot bear to come out with it – and let it seep out in odd symptomatic ways. In sly and unfair ways, they seek to push us to take the agonising next step.

On the other hand, there is so much that can spare us excessive pain at the end:

Directness
Kind departing lovers make a sharp break. It's awful, of course, but there's a vein of mature kindness in their brusque manner: in an obviously difficult situation, they are sparing us the extended torture of false hope.

Reasons
Good departing lovers try to explain in convincing ways why the relationship didn't work out. They're not saying you are horrendous or a fool – just that the two of you turn out not to be very adept partners for each other.

Honesty about who they are

Nice departing lovers let us see and actively remind us of what's not so nice or good about them. They admit that they brought a lot of difficult things into the relationship. They are doing us the kindness of showing us that life with them would be seriously difficult in major ways. We're losing them, but we're not losing the prospect of a blissful or problem-free future.

Honesty about who we are

Without being aggressive or mean, good departing lovers give us a fair picture of why, in fact, they found it hard to be around us in the end. This is hard news, but it's also very constructive. We're going to have to take this into account in the future if other relationships are to go better.

Being hated

Good departing lovers know that the news they are breaking will, inevitably, lead to them being hated for a time. They are sanguine and brave in the face of this. They don't suffer from the fateful and sentimental desire to be loved by people they no longer love.

We're gradually disentangling two distinct sources of pain – which mean very different things. There's the sorrow of losing someone we liked. But there may well also be the suffering caused by the unfortunate ways a lover acted at the end – which tells us about them, but not really about us. We may not be able to escape the agony of broken hearts, but we can always strive to keep it to a very basic minimum.

Infidelity

Infidelity is commonly interpreted as close to the greatest tragedy that could befall any relationship, and as the natural, inevitable prelude to the break-up of a union.

It is viewed in such dark terms because, under the philosophy of Romanticism, which has dominated our understanding of love since the middle of the 18th century, sex is understood to be not principally a physical act but the summation and central symbol of love. Before Romanticism, people had sex and fell in love, but they did not always see these two acts as inextricably linked: one might love someone and not sleep with them, or sleep with them and not love them. It was this dislocation that Romanticism refused to countenance. Sex was simply the crowning moment of love, the superlative way of expressing one's devotion to someone, the ultimate proof of one's sincerity.

What this philosophy unwittingly accomplished was to turn infidelity from a problem into a catastrophe. Never again could sex be viewed as being divorced from intense emotion and a profound desire for commitment. It was no longer possible to say that sex meant 'nothing', in the sense of being a joyful, kind but emotionally empty act devoid of any desire to care for or live with a new person in the long term and in no way indicative of any drop in affection for the established partner. There are, of course, many cases where infidelity means exactly what Romanticism takes it to mean: contempt for one's relationship. But in many other cases, it may mean something rather different: a passing, surface desire for erotic excitement that coexists with an ongoing, sincere commitment to one's life partner.

Our culture makes this thought close to impossible, so 'getting over' an infidelity – by which is meant, learning to see that the unfaithful act might not mean what Romanticism tells us it means – has become a challenge of heroic proportions and, most of the time, a brute impossibility. However much an unfaithful partner may patiently explain that it meant nothing, the idea seems entirely implausible. How could sex, the summation of love, ever mean anything less than pretty much everything?

There may be one potential way out of the impasse: a frank examination of the recesses of one's own mind and, perhaps, an honest recall of certain moments of past personal experience. What this brave investigation is likely to throw up is evidence that one is strangely capable of something rather surprising: caring deeply for someone and yet entertaining, or masterminding, a sexual scenario involving somebody else. However much the thought seems unbelievable when we hear it from the mouth of a straying partner, in some ways it seems quite possible to think of having sex with one person and loving another.

The best way to recover after an infidelity may therefore be to ignore what Romanticism tells us that infidelity has to mean, and to consult a more reliable source of information: what we ourselves took infidelity to mean the last time the idea crossed through our minds. It is on this basis that we may – with considerable pain, of course – come to be able to forgive and even in a way understand and accept the apologies of a repentant partner. It is on the basis of subjective experience of unfaithful thoughts that we may redemptively enrich, complicate and soften what happens when we end up as their victims.

Kissing

Why is kissing so significant and potentially so exciting?

Sexual excitement is psychological. It's not so much what our bodies happen to be doing that is getting us so turned on. It's what's happening in our brains that matters.

Partly the excitement of kissing is the result of social codes. The huge meaning of kissing is something we've built up by social agreement and its fundamental definition is: I accept you – accept you so much that I will take a big risk with you. It is on this basis that kissing isn't merely physically nice, but psychologically delightful.

Kissing is exciting because it could so easily be revolting. The inside of a mouth is deeply private. No one usually goes there outside of the dentist. It's yours alone. The thought of the mouth of someone you don't like is properly creepy. Ordinarily it would be utterly nauseating to have a stranger poke their tongue into your face; the idea of their saliva lubricating your lips is horrendous. So to allow someone to do these things signals a huge level of acceptance. There's a special joy of touching someone's back teeth with your tongue, which has nothing to do with the appeal of licking enamel. All of us suffer from strong feelings of unacceptability and shame, which another's kiss starts to work on overcoming.

Apart from the public overt person, everyone has a more elusive, deeper self, which is kept in reserve as far as other people are concerned, and yet is hugely familiar from the inside. This deeper, private self is active in a serious kiss; which is what you feel you are getting and giving access to. In the kiss, our mouth becomes a privileged place in which we surrender our defences and gift ourselves to another. We are properly exposed and raw. Kissing promises something far more exciting still than sex: a brief respite from loneliness.

Long-Distance Love

When we hear that a couple live eleven time zones apart and can afford to come together only once in a long while, it's natural to offer sympathy for the pain. We should more fairly envy them for their luck.

Whatever our longings may indicate, it is simply a lot easier to love someone who isn't there. Far from an unfortunate necessity, living apart should be recognised for what it truly is: an advantage.

So much goes right when we live a long way away:

– Online or over the phone, we never assume that the other person should be able to read our minds without us having explained what is in them. We accept that we will have to describe our days, as well as our desires, in words and pictures. We can't help but do that thing that holds couples together: communicate.

– We accept that the other can live without us – and therefore make the effort to be the sort of people someone would freely choose to be with.

– We never have to find out how much it can tarnish love to be with someone who has a different idea of how to organise a cutlery drawer or the correct way to suspend a towel.

– Apart, we can sample the gentle suffering of loneliness over the intense rage of suffocation.

– We can benefit from what jealousy otherwise prevents us from admitting: how much it helps us to feel like desirable, potent people to be able to go out and flirt with someone else for a while without too many questions being asked. In other words, how profoundly loyal a whiff of surface disloyalty helps us to be.

– We appreciate more. It's a strange quirk of our minds, but we only ever notice what's missing: the money we don't have; the weather we long for; the car we don't yet own. Yet, once anything is securely in our possession, it disappears. The best way to lose ownership of something is to own it – and the surest way to forget your partner exists may be to ensure they're beside you every night.

And yet, without ever meaning to do so, the long-distance relationship may simply, despite all its evident challenges, throw up some of the absolutely ideal conditions for true love to thrive. We should be wise to imbibe a few of the lessons life normally only teaches us when they're in Sydney and we're in Vancouver – and carefully import them into our lives, even with the people unfortunate enough to be right next to us.

Long-Term Love

Much of our collective thinking about love targets the problems we face around starting a relationship. To the Romantic, love essentially means *finding love*. What we blithely call a love story is mostly, in fact, the start of a love story.

Yet the true, heroic challenges of love are concerned with how to keep love going over the long term, in the face of hurdles not generally discussed in art and, as a result, lacking glamour: incompatible work schedules, differing ideas about bathroom etiquette, phone calls with ex-partners, waning lust, the demands of household management, business trips that clash with anniversaries, the question of whether and when to have children, divergent parenting styles, problematic in-laws and economic stresses.

To negotiate these challenges, long-term love requires us to develop a host of skills that our societies tend to stay quiet about: forgiveness, charity, humour, imagination and seeing the other as a loveable idiot (rather than simply a disappointment). To love over time involves striving to understand what another person is really trying to say when they are upset, even if what they are uttering is on the surface shockingly disdainful. It might involve discovering the dignity of domestic chores or a melancholy acceptance that a good relationship might require the sacrifice of certain dreams of sexual fulfilment. We'll have to say sorry even if we are not really at fault; we'll have to tell many little white lies and occasionally rather large ones; we'll have to face the fact that we'll discover some grim shortcomings in the other person, and they in us.

Realistic, scratchy, long-term love is diametrically at odds with the Romantic vision of being in love. Therefore, by the standards of Romantic love, it has to look like an unfolding catastrophe. Far from it: it is what naturally happens when love is reciprocated and when decent, normal people live side by side for a long time. It is part of what good ordinary relationships look like over the years. It is what happens when love succeeds.

Love as
Education

At the heart of the Romantic vision of love is an idea of complete mutual acceptance. To seek to change one's lover feels like a profound offence against the whole idea of love.

This way of thinking about and experiencing love can feel entirely natural, but it is a relatively recent historical invention. It stands in sharp contrast to a much older, and in certain ways wiser, view: the Classical idea that love is an arena of growth and change. This view of love was developed in Ancient Greece, prompted particularly by the philosophical ideas of Socrates and Plato. As they saw it, the task of love is first and foremost to educate one's lover. We don't love someone because we think they are perfect already, but because we can see what they could be; we love their potential and their emergent (but not yet fully developed) qualities. Their deep attachment to us means that we have an ideal opportunity for guiding and shaping their development towards the articulation of their full potential. Love is a mutually supportive structure in which two people can guide one another to their respective virtuous ideal selves.

This pedagogical view of love now sounds extremely odd. We don't imagine love as a classroom. Our current culture imagines the lover as a great admirer. Classical culture imagined them as a great teacher – the person best fitted to edge us towards becoming who we should be. We are suspicious because we think of teaching in the guise of nagging: the pure demand for change, rather than an eloquent enticement to surrender our entrenched flaws.

Love as
Generosity

To fall in love with someone is typically assumed to involve awe at a person's physical and psychological virtues. We think of ourselves as 'in love' when we are bewitched by a rare creature who seems in myriad ways stronger and more accomplished than we are; our love seems founded on admiration.

But there is another view of love that deserves to be explored; a philosophy of love founded on generosity. From this perspective, to love means not only or primarily to experience admiration in the face of perfection; it involves a capacity to be uncommonly generous towards a fellow human at moments when they may be less than straightforwardly appealing. Love is taken to mean not a thrill in the face of accomplishment, but a distinctive skill founded on the ability to see beyond a person's off-putting outer dimensions, an energy to enter imaginatively into their experiences and bestow an ongoing degree of forgiveness and kindness in spite of marked trickiness and confusion.

Love as Generosity

Love Me as I Am

Our culture strongly inclines us to the view that genuine love must involve complete acceptance of another person in their good and especially somewhat bad sides. In moments of fury with our partners, we may be tempted to dismiss their complaints against us with the cry: 'Love me as I am.'

But in truth, none of us should want to remain exactly as we are – and therefore none of us should too strongly want another person to love (as opposed to tolerate or simply forgive) what is warped within us.

Genuine love might be defined as gently and kindly helping someone to become the best version of themselves rather than accepting them precisely as they are. It isn't a betrayal of love for someone to try to help us evolve or to teach us to be better people; it may be the highest proof of genuine commitment.

Unfortunately, under the sway of Romantic ideology that makes us suspicious of emotional education, most of us end up being terrible teachers and equally terrible students. We don't accept the legitimacy, let alone nobility, of others' desires to teach us, and can't acknowledge areas where we might need to be taught. We rebel against the very structure of a lover's education that would enable criticism to be moulded into sensible-sounding lessons and to be heard as caring attempts to rejig the more trou-blesome aspects of our personalities.

At the first sign that the other is adopting a teacherly tone, we tend to assume that we are being 'attacked' and betrayed. We therefore close our ears to the instruction, reacting with sarcasm and aggression to the teacher.

Our stance is deeply understandable: to the mother, ev-erything about the tiny infant is delightful; they wouldn't change even the smallest thing; their baby is perfect just as it is. Our idea of love has taken this attitude to heart: it's what (we think) love is supposed to be like. The suggestion that another could change, grow, or improve is taken as an insult to love.

The problem is: the mother never in fact loved us just as we were. She hoped we would keep growing up. And the need is still there. Our bodies may be fully formed, but our psyches always have some way to go. We shouldn't hold it against our lovers if they don't love us as we are, if they'd sweetly like us to be a bit different.

Loving and
Being Loved

Curiously, we speak of love as one thing rather than discerning the two very different varieties that lie beneath a single word: being loved and loving. It appears that we can only make a relationship work properly when we are ready to do the latter and are aware of our unnatural, immature fixation on the former.

We start knowing only about being loved. It comes to seem very wrongly like the norm. To the child, it feels as if the parent is simply spontaneously on hand to comfort, guide, entertain, feed and clear up while remaining almost always warm and cheerful. The parents don't reveal how often they've bitten their tongue, fought back tears, and been too tired to take off their clothes after a day of childcare.

We learn of love in an entirely non-reciprocal context. The parent loves but they don't expect the favour to be returned in any significant way. The parent doesn't get upset when the child doesn't notice a new haircut or ask carefully calibrated questions about how the meeting at work went or suggest that the parent go upstairs and take a much-needed nap. Parent and child may both love, but each party is on a very different end of the axis – unbeknownst to the child.

This is why in adulthood when we first say that we long for love, what we predominantly mean is that we want to be loved as we were once loved by a parent. We want a re-creation in adulthood of what it felt like to be administered to and indulged. In a secret part of our minds, we picture someone who will understand our needs, bring us what we want, be immensely sympathetic and patient towards us, act selflessly and make many things better.

Naturally, this is a disaster for our unions. For any relationship to work, we need to move firmly out of the position of the child and into that of the parent. We need to become someone who can sometimes subordinate their own demands to the needs of another.

To be adults in love, we have to learn – perhaps for the very first time – to do something truly remarkable: to put someone else ahead of us, for a time at least. That's what true, mature love actually is, much to everyone's initial surprise.

Monogamy

To a greater extent than we perhaps realise, when it comes to what sort of relationship we are allowed to have, our societies present us with a menu with only a single option on it: the monogamous, cohabiting romantic relationship, usually served with a side order of children.

But what is striking, for an arrangement that is supposed to be entirely normal, is just how many people cannot abide by its rules. Around half flunk completely, and a substantial portion muddle along in quiet desperation.

In our societies, those who can't get on with Romantic monogamous marriage are quickly diagnosed as suffering from a variety of psychological disorders: fear of intimacy, clinginess, sexual addiction, frigidity, boundary issues, self-sabotage, childhood trauma, etc.

But there might be another approach, this one drawn from the pioneering work of advocates of LGBTQIA+ rights, namely that any taste or proclivity must by definition be acceptable and non-pathological, except in so far as it might hurt the unwilling or unconsenting. From this perspective, while many ways of life might be different to society's presently preferred option, it cannot be right to judge, correct, amend and seek to re-educate all those attracted to them.

In love, we accept an absence of choice that would be intolerable in other areas of life. We consent to wearing a uniform that cannot possibly fit our varied shapes, and without daring to make even minor moves to assemble our own wardrobe. All our collective energies go into creating astonishing varieties of foods, machines and entertainment, while the entity that dominates our lives – our relationships – continue in a format more or less unchanged for 200 years.

It would be a genuine liberation if, whenever a new couple came together, it was assumed that they almost certainly would not go along with the Romantic monogamous template, and that the onus was therefore on them to discuss – up front, in good faith and without insult – the arrangements that would ideally satisfy their natures.

Once upon a time, male offspring of the European upper classes had only two career options: to join the army or to join the church. Such narrow-mindedness was eventually dismissed as evident nonsense and eradicated, and the average citizen of a developed country now has thousands of job options to choose from. We should strive for a comparable expansion of our menus of love. We are not so much bad at relationships, as unable – presently – to understand our needs without shame, to stick up politely for what makes us content, and to invent practical arrangements that could stand a chance of honouring our complex emotional reality.

Romantic Disappointment

Often our partner isn't terrible in any big way, but we feel a growing sadness about our relationship: they're not as focused on us as we'd hoped; they don't understand us fully; they're preoccupied, a bit abrupt, not hugely interested in the details of our day; they call their friends rather than talk with us. We feel disenchanted and let down, and may start to think we're with the wrong person.

This sorrow has a paradoxical source: early childhood. At the best moments of childhood, a loving parent offered us extraordinary satisfaction. They knew when we were hungry or tired, even though we couldn't explain. They made us feel completely safe. They were enchanted by our smallest achievements. We were entertained and indulged.

As adults, we continue to be in thrall to this notion of being loved, and find our partners sorely wanting as a result. It's a natural but profoundly unfair comparison. Our needs were so much simpler then. We didn't need someone to trawl intelligently through the troubled corners of our minds and understand why it is necessary to see our aunt on Sunday, why it matters to us that the curtains harmonise with the sofa covers, or why bread must be cut with a proper bread knife. Our partner is stumbling in the dark around needs that are immensely subtle, far from obvious and very complicated to deliver on.

The source of our present sorrow is not, therefore, that our adult lovers are tragically inept or uniquely selfish. It's rather that we're judging our adult experiences in the light of a very different kind of childhood love. We are sorrowful not because we have landed with the wrong person, but because we have grown up.

Romantic
Instinct

For most of history, relationships were a rational business, to do with matching land, status and religion. Marriages were cold, ruthless and almost wholly disconnected from the happiness of their protagonists.

What replaced the Marriage of Reason was the Marriage of Instinct, an arrangement that dictated that feeling should be the supreme guide to the formation of good relationships. Passionate emotion became viewed as the ideal predictor of fifty years of conjugal happiness.

We have grown used to following our hearts. Unfortunately, only too often, these hearts prove troublingly deceptive and unreliable. Our instincts pull us not so much towards situations that will make us happy as situations that feel familiar, which might be quite a different thing.

This is because adult love intimately rehearses the themes of childhood love, and a great many of us learnt of love in childhood in less-than-ideal conditions. The love we tasted when we were small will likely have involved not only tenderness and affection but also (in some form or other) troublesome dynamics: there might have been depression, anger, withdrawal, abandonment, favouritism, a pressure to succeed, or a subtle call to fail.

When we reach adulthood, our 'instinct' then has a habit of impelling us towards situations that echo the less-than-ideal themes of childhood: we seek to find people of similar emotional maturity to our childhood caregivers. This explains why we so often find ourselves rejecting candidates who might on paper be eminently well matched and mature. Yet we cannot muster enthusiasm and complain that they are 'boring' or 'not sexy'. What we may at a subliminal level mean is: simply not disturbed enough to make us suffer in the ways we need to suffer in order to feel that love is real.

The time has come to outgrow our veneration of 'instinct'. We need relationships in which our feelings have been properly submitted to examination and brought under the aegis of a mature awareness of our long and always distinctively troubled psychological histories.

Secrets

Our ideal of Romantic love has at its heart the notion that a truly good relationship is one in which we are able to tell a partner everything.

At last, there will be no more need for the usual hypocrisies. We will be able to come clean about so much that we had previously needed to keep to ourselves: our reservations about our friends; our irritation over small but wounding remarks by colleagues; our interest in rarely mentioned sexual practices.

Love seems founded on the idea of radical disclosure. But gradually, we stand to become aware of so much we cannot say. It might be around sex: on a work trip we flirted with a colleague and nearly let our hand touch theirs; we discovered a porn site that beautifully targeted a special quirk of our erotic imagination; we find our partner's brother or sister very alluring. Or the secret thoughts can be more broad-ranging: the blog they wrote for work, about their experience in client care, was very boring; they are putting on weight around their waist; their best friend from school, to whom they are still loyal, is (in our view) excessively silly and dull; in the wedding photo of their parents (lovingly displayed in a silver frame in the living room) their mother looks very smug.

Love begins with a hope of unburdening ourselves entirely and overcoming loneliness forever. The initial relief of honesty is at the heart of the feeling of being 'in love'. But this sharing of secrets sets up in our minds – and in our collective culture – a hugely problematic ideal: that if two people love one another, they must always tell each other the truth about everything.

The idea of honesty is sublime. It presents a deeply moving vision of how two people can be together, and it is a constant presence in the early months. But in order to be kind, and in order to sustain love, it ultimately becomes necessary to keep many thoughts out of sight.

Keeping secrets can seem like a betrayal of the relationship. At the same time, the complete truth invariably places any union in mortal danger. Much of what we'd ideally like to have recognised and confirmed is going to be genuinely disturbing even to someone who is fond of us.

We face a choice between honesty and acceptability, and – for reasons that deserve a great deal of sympathy – mostly we choose the latter. We are perhaps too conscious of the bad reasons for hiding something; we haven't paid enough attention to the noble reasons why, from time to time, true loyalty may lead us to say very much less than the whole truth. We are so impressed by honesty that we have forgotten the virtues of politeness – this word defined not as a cynical withholding of important information for the sake of harm, but as a dedication to not rubbing someone else up against the true, hurtful aspects of our nature. It is ultimately no great sign of kindness to insist on showing someone our entire selves at all times. Repression, a certain degree of restraint and a dedication to editing our pronouncements belong to love as much as a capacity for explicit confession. The person who cannot tolerate secrets, who in the name of 'being honest' divulges information so wounding it cannot be forgotten, is no friend of love. We should accept an ongoing need to edit our full reality.

Self-Love

One of the great and slightly strange dangers of falling in love with someone is how we may respond the day they start to love us back.

Some of the reasons we fall in love with people is because we long to escape from ourselves into the embrace of a person who appears as beautiful, perfect and accomplished as we feel ourselves to be flawed, dumb and mediocre. But what if such a being were to one day turn around and love us back? Nothing could discredit them faster. How could they be as divine as we had hoped when they have the bad taste to approve of someone like us?

It turns out that one of the central requirements of a good relationship is a degree of affection for ourselves; built up over the years, largely in childhood. We need a legacy of feeling deserving of love in order not to respond very obtusely to the affections granted to us by adult partners. Without a decent amount of self-love, the love of another person will always prove sickening and misguided, and we will self-destructively – though unconsciously – set out to repel or disappoint it. It will simply feel more normal and therefore comfortable to be disliked or ignored when that is mostly what we have known.

If we are not wholly convinced of our own lovability, receiving affection can appear like being bestowed a prize for an accomplishment we don't feel we ever earned. People unfortunate enough to fall in love with self-hating types must brace themselves for the recriminations due to all false flatterers.

There is the old joke made by the American comedian and actor Groucho Marx about not deigning to belong to a club that would accept someone like him as a member. We laugh at the Marxist position because of its absurd contradictions: how is it possible that we should both wish to join a club, and yet lose that wish as soon as it comes true? Why wouldn't we just be happy to have been allowed into a club?

The answer lies in self-hatred; because for many of us, being accepted into a grand and beautiful club doesn't feel like what our inner psyches have been shaped to accept. We wonder how we can continue to believe in the club, or indeed the beloved, now that they believe in us.

There is usually a troubling Marxist moment in every relationship, a moment when it becomes clear that love is going to be reciprocated; that we won't simply admire someone from afar without hope of mutuality. The way it is resolved depends on the balance between self-love and self-hatred. If self-hatred gains the upper hand, then the one who is being loved back will declare that the beloved (on some excuse or other) is not good enough for them (not good enough by virtue of associating with no-goods).

But if self-love gains the upper hand, then both partners may accept that seeing their love reciprocated is not proof of how low the beloved is, but of how lovable they have themselves turned out to be. It turns out that knowing how to love ourselves a little can be one of the kindest and therefore most romantic things we can ever learn to do for our partners.

Sex

One of the great burdens that our Romantic culture has imposed upon long-term relationships is the idea that, if things are working as they should, love and sexual fulfilment must always fit neatly together.

This beautiful and hugely convenient idea raises a passionate hope that over many years two people will not only like and help one another, manage their domestic finances reasonably well, perhaps raise a family, have enjoyable holidays, understand one another's problems, schedule cleaning rotas, put up with each other's failings, see each other's parents and friends and pursue their careers in harmony, but they will also be devoted and exciting sexual partners, endlessly entwining and recombining, sometimes being gentle and slow, at others, brutal and urgent, travelling together on a shared, life-long erotic adventure.

It is this sublime idea that begins to torment us when – as is the case in almost every relationship – sex gradually becomes less intense and less frequent, more cautious and more frustrating, more at odds with daily life and eventually more daunting as a prospect than reading a book, watching the news together or simply going to sleep. This can appear nothing short of a catastrophe, a sign of monstrous failure and very often a prelude to a break-up.

Yet the problem is not ours alone. It is simply that almost everything that can make love go well seems primed not to make sex go well, and vice versa. We are afflicted by a fundamental misalignment in the qualities of character and spirit required by good sex on the one hand and successful love on the other. A relationship cannot survive in the long term without tenderness, soberness, practical intelligence and selective resignation. We have to carefully fathom another's motives, explain our moods, overcome hurts and sulks and assume a mantle of predictability.

Sex, on the other hand, in its most dramatic, thrilling versions, demands that we be heedless, decadent, perhaps cruel or untenably submissive. It can involve the crudest language and moments of beautiful, tender degradation. In having to suffer from feelings of inadequacy around what happens in long-term love, we are the victims of major cultural failure: the failure of our surrounding culture to continually stress a realistic picture of an unavoidable tension between two crucial yet incompatible themes of existence.

In a wiser world, we would collectively admit that the very rare cases where love and sex did run together were astonishing exceptions with no relevance to the majority of lives. We would instead learn to pay admiring attention to those who had accepted with a reasonable show of dignity and grace that the natural price of long-term togetherness is a decline in the quality and frequency of sexual contact – and that this is, in many cases, a price worth paying.

Splitting and
Integration

The pioneering mid-20th-century Viennese psychoanalyst Melanie Klein drew attention to something very dramatic that happens in the minds of babies during feeding sessions with their mothers. When feeding goes well, the baby is blissfully happy and sees mummy as 'good'. But if, for whatever reason, the feeding process is difficult, the baby can't grasp that it is dealing with the same person it liked a lot only a few hours ago. It splits off from the actual mother a second, 'bad' version, whom it deems to be a separate, hateful individual, responsible for deliberately frustrating its wishes, and in the process, protecting the image of the good mother in its mind.

Gradually, if things go well, there follows a long and difficult process by which the child integrates these two different people and comes, sadly but realistically, to grasp that there is no ideal, 'perfect' mummy – just one person who is usually lovely but can also be cross, busy, tired, who can make mistakes, and be very interested in other people.

It may have been a long time since we were being fed as babies, but the tendency to 'split' those close to us is always there, for we never fully outgrow our childhood selves. In adult life, we may fall deeply in love and split off an ideal version of someone, in whom we see no imperfections and whom we adore without limit. Yet we may suddenly and violently turn against the partner (or a celebrity or a politician) whose good qualities once impressed us the moment we discover the slightest thing that disturbs or frustrates us in them. We may conclude that they cannot really be good since they have made us suffer.

We may find it extremely hard to accept that the same person might be very nice and good in some ways and strikingly disappointing in others. The bad version can appear to destroy the good one, although these are really just different and connected aspects of one complex person.

To cope with the conflict between hope and reality, our culture should teach us good integration skills, prompting us to accept what is imperfect in ourselves and others. We should be gently reminded that no one we can love will ever satisfy us completely, but that it is never worth hating them on that score alone. We should move from the naivety and rage of splitting to the mature wisdom of integration.

Sulking

Sulking combines a powerful symbolic articulation of anger with an intense desire not to communicate what one is angry about. We both desperately need to be understood and yet we are profoundly committed to not making it easy for another person to understand us.

The stance is no coincidence. We remain silent and furiously gnomic because having to spell out the offence another has caused feels contrary to the spirit of love, interpreted in a Romantic sense: if the other requires an explanation, it is proof they are not worthy of being granted one. After all, true love should be about mutual speedy intuition, not laborious articulation.

In a sense, it is an odd privilege to be the recipient of a sulk, for we tend to fall into a sulk only with people whom we feel should understand us, in whom we have placed a high degree of trust, and yet who appear to have broken the contract of the relationship. We would never dare to storm out of a room, call someone a shit and stay silent the rest of the evening in an upstairs room unless we were with a partner whom we believed had a profound capacity to understand us, which they had – strangely, probably out of spite – chosen not to use on this occasion. It is one of the stranger gifts of love.

Sulking pays homage to a beautiful, yet in practice catastrophic, Romantic ideal of love: that of being understood without needing to speak. At a deep level, the structure of the sulk reveals a debt to earliest childhood. In the womb, we never had to explain what we needed. Food and comfort simply came. If we had the privilege of being relatively well parented, some of that idyll may have continued in our first years. We didn't have to make our every need known; someone guessed for us. They saw through our tears, our inarticulacy, our confusions, and found the explanations when we didn't have the ability to verbalise them. The sulker continues to want to be interpreted the way they once were.

The cure is a dose of pessimism. We should be reminded of the unfairness of wanting every aspect of our souls to be grasped without us needing to say a word. It is not necessarily an insult to be misunderstood and called upon to communicate. When our lovers fail to fathom us and unwittingly barge into our more tender sides, it isn't an immediate sign that they are heartless. It may merely be that we have grown a little too committed to not teaching them about who we are.

The Happy Single

One of the most important principles for choosing a lover sensibly is not to feel in any hurry to make a choice. Being satisfied with being single is a precondition of satisfactory coupledom. We cannot choose wisely when remaining single feels unbearable. We have to be utterly at peace with the prospect of many years of solitude in order to have any chance of forming a good relationship. Or we'll love no longer being single rather more than we love the partner who spared us being so.

Unfortunately, after a certain age, society makes single-hood feel dangerously unpleasant. Communal life starts to wither. People in couples are too threatened by the independence of the single to invite them around very often – in case they are reminded of something they might have missed. Friendship and sex are, despite all the gadgets, remarkably hard to come by. No wonder that when some-one even slightly decent comes along, we cling to them, to our eventual enormous cost.

When sex was only available within marriage, people recognised that this led people to marry for the wrong rea-sons: to obtain something that was artificially restricted in society as a whole. Sexual liberation was intended to allow people to have a clearer head when choosing who they really wanted to be with. But the process remains only half-finished. Only when we make sure that being single can be potentially as secure, warm and fulfilling as being in a couple will we know that people are choosing to pair up for the right reasons. It's time to liberate 'companionship' from the shackles of coupledom, and make it as widely and as easily available as sexual liberators wanted sex to be.

In the meantime, we should strive to make ourselves as much at peace as we can with the idea of being alone for a very long time. Only then do we stand a chance of deciding to be with someone on the basis of their own and true merits.

Unrequited
Love

For intense periods of our lives, we suffer the agony of unrequited love. Our sorrow is accompanied by a certainty that if only the elusive being would return our smiles, come for dinner or marry us, we would know bliss. Epochal happiness seems tantalisingly close, wholly real and yet maddeningly out of reach.

At such moments, we are often counselled to try to forget the beloved. Given their lack of interest, we should try to think of something or someone else. Yet this kindness is deeply misguided. The cure for love does not lie in ceasing to think of the fugitive lover, but in learning to think more intensely and constructively about who they might really be.

From close up, every human who has ever lived proves deeply challenging. At close quarters, we are all trying propositions. We are short-tempered, vain, deceitful, crass, sentimental, woolly, over- or under-emotional and chaotic. What prevents us from holding this in mind in relation to certain people is simply a lack of knowledge. On the basis of a few charming outside details, we assume that the target of our passion may miraculously have escaped the fundamentals of the human condition.

They haven't. We just haven't got to know them properly. This is what makes unrequited love so intense, so long-lasting and so vicious. By preventing us from properly growing close to them, the beloved also prevents us from tiring of them in the cathartic and liberating manner that is the gift of requited love. It isn't their charms that are keeping us magnetised; it is our lack of knowledge of their flaws.

The cure for unrequited love is, in structure, therefore very simple: we must get to know them better. The more we discover of them, the less they would look like the solution to all our problems. We would discover the endless small ways in which they were irksome; we'd get to know how stubborn, how critical, how cold and how hurt by things that strike us as meaningless they could be. If we got to know them better, we would realise how much they had in common with everyone else.

Passion can never withstand too much exposure to the full reality of another person. The unbounded admiration on which it is founded is destroyed by the knowledge that a properly shared life inevitably brings.

The cruelty of unrequited love isn't really that we haven't been loved back; it's that our hopes have been aroused by someone who can never disappoint us, someone who we will have to keep believing in because we lack the knowledge that would set us free.

In the absence of a direct cure, we must undertake an imaginative one. Without quite knowing the details, we must accept that they would eventually prove decisively irritating. Everyone does. We have to believe this, not because we know it exactly of them, but because they are human, and we know this dark but deeply cheering fact about everyone who has ever lived.

Also available from The School of Life:

Essential Ideas: Self-Awareness

**From the new pocket book series, featuring key ideas from
The School of Life exploring self-awareness.**

Understanding ourselves is the key to unlocking our true potential.

Here is a collection of The School of Life's most penetrating insights into the puzzles of self-awareness. This book teaches us how to look into ourselves, how to make sense of our past and how to overcome anxiety and confusion.

In a highly compressed and entertaining form, The School of Life introduces us to a person we've been in flight from for too long and will benefit hugely from getting to know: our deep selves.

ISBN: 978-1-916753-02-0

Essential Ideas: Serenity

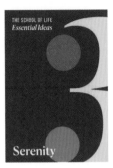

**From the new pocket book series, featuring key ideas from
The School of Life exploring serenity.**

Knowing how to fight off anxiety and remain calm belong to the greatest
skills we can ever aspire to. Only with a serene state of mind are we in
any position to enjoy all the other good things in life: friendship, love,
family or work.

Here is a selection of The School of Life's finest essays on the art of
serenity. They teach us how to achieve the correct perspective on our
problems, how to understand the worst of our fears and how to surround
ourselves with the sort of people who can help us in our quest for a less
anxious existence.

We have – most of us – already spent far too long on needless worry;
here at last is a crucial guide to the less turbulent future we deserve.

ISBN: 978-1-916753-26-6

To join The School of Life community and find out more,
scan below:

The School of Life publishes a range of books on essential topics
in psychological and emotional life, including relationships,
parenting, friendship, careers and fulfilment. The aim is always to
help us to understand ourselves better and thereby to grow calmer,
less confused and more purposeful. Discover our full range of
titles, including books for children, here:
www.theschooloflife.com/books

The School of Life also offers a comprehensive therapy service,
which complements, and draws upon, our published works:
www.theschooloflife.com/therapy

THESCHOOLOFLIFE.COM